MACHINES ON THE MOVE

SEMIS

by Natalie Deniston

TABLE OF CONTENTS

Tadpole Books, an imprint of Jump! Library by FlutterBee

tadpole books

WORDS TO KNOW

cab

driver

pulls

tractor

trailer

wheels

SEMIS

A semi is a truck.

It is big.

wheel

It has 18 wheels!

A tractor is in front.

It pulls a trailer.

Boxes go in.

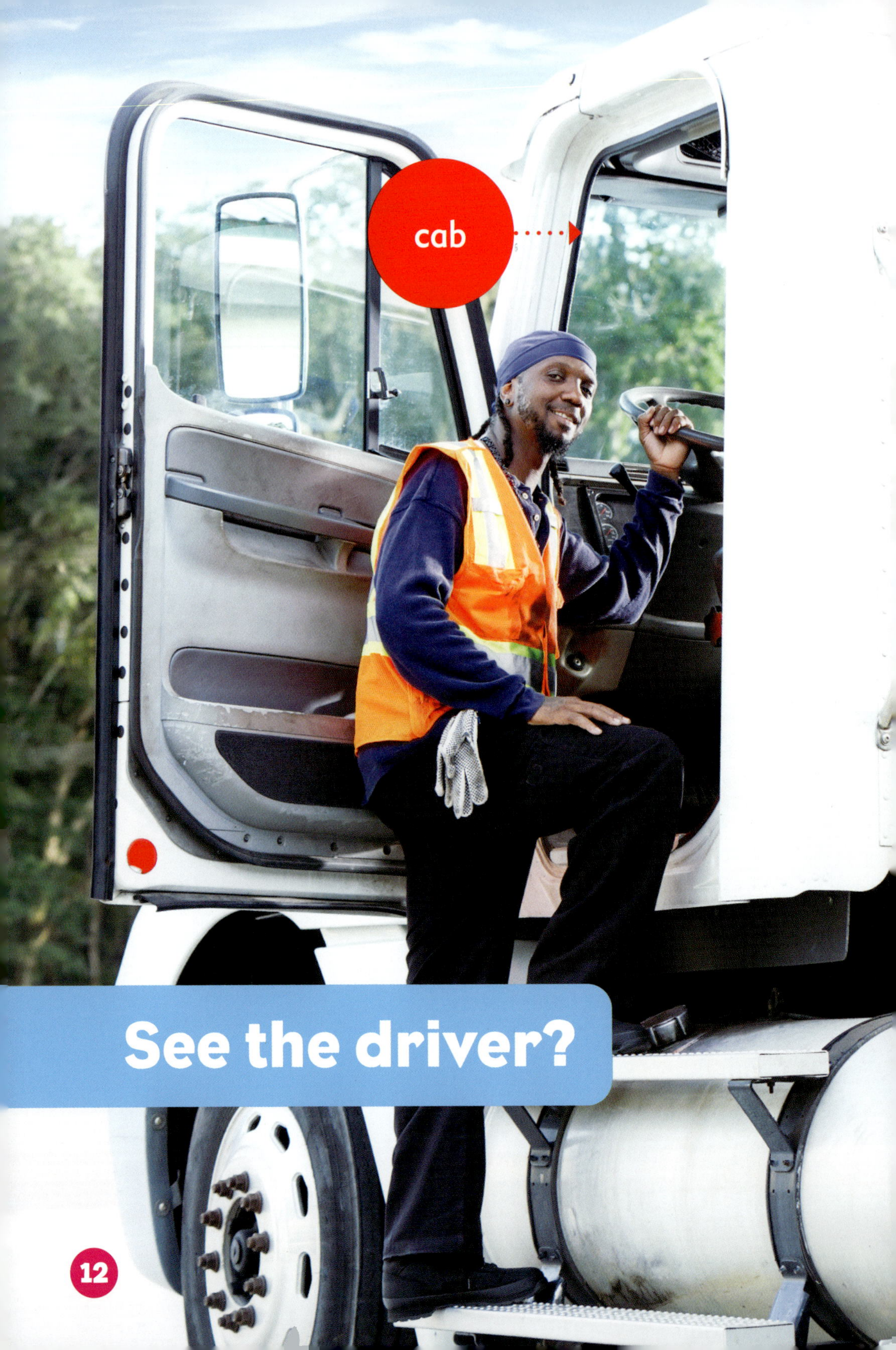

See the driver?

He gets in the cab.

Watch them go!

LET'S REVIEW!

Semis carry and move things we need. What parts of a semi can you name?

INDEX